DRAGON WAIF

A Selection of Sketches from the Other Side of My Soul

DRAGON WAIF

A Selection of Sketches from the Other Side of My Soul

V. A. MATATUMUA VERMEULEN

Published by Hyacinthus Books™ an imprint of Island Ink Publishing Co. Ltd. 71-75 Shelton Street, Covent Garden, London, WC2H 9JQ, United Kingdom.

ISBN 978-1-914093-00-5 (Paperback)
ISBN 978-1-914093-01-2 (Hard Cover)

A CIP catalogue record for this book is available from the British Library.

Names: Matatumua Vermeulen, Vincent Albert also known as Vermeulen, Vincent Albert 1969 – author

Title: Dragon Waif. A Selection of Sketches from the Other Side of My Soul | Vincent Albert Matatumua Vermeulen also known as Vincent Albert Vermeulen

Description: Poetry

Subjects: BISAC: POE 021000 POETRY / LGBT, POE023010 POETRY / Subjects & Themes / Death, Grief, Loss, POE023020 POETRY / Subjects & Themes / Love & Erotica, POE 010000 POETRY/ Australia & Oceania.

Dragon Waif is dedicated to my patron God Apollo Musa'getes.

And to my Friends who believed and encouraged me when everyone else was doing the opposite.

Those friends thou hast, and their adoption tried,
Grapple them to thy soul with hoops of steel;

Polonius to Larates Act 1 Scene 3
The Tragedy of Hamlet, Prince of Denmark
William Shakespeare

"Every secret of a writer's soul, every experience of his life, every quality of his mind, is written large in his works."

Virginia Woolf.

CONTENTS

DRAGON WAIF

A Selection of Sketches from the Other Side of My Soul

1: RAIN

Rain is beautiful
In any form
Rain is beautiful
Even in a storm.

1982.

2: IF

If it was raining icy diamonds
upon an earth-lit moonscape
with purple snowflakes
upon valleys of red sand dunes
the plains of Venus
with Saturn's rainbow rings
moonshine irridiant[1]
scintillating
upon a violet lake
would you . . . ?

30/09/90.

---

[1] Poetic license to use the word "irridiant" issued by Clem Matheson.

3: LIKE CAESAR

Oh soul of darkness
In sorrow weeping
For trust betrayed
Echo, Caesar's words
In stunned silence
Sadness deepening
At betrayal's wound
Fearful, of losing friendship
Confused, uncertain
Aching soul
In darkness floundering
in darkness drowning
like Caesar's death
demanding:
ET TU BRUTE!?

21/05/91.

4. DAWN

Dawn breaks to a leaden sea
Cold and heavy
Beneath an iron clad sky.
The raging surf, now muted,
Frothing sea-lace
Along a shore swept clean
And strewn with coral treasures,
Couched in fresh seaweed.
The piercing cries of gulls
Winging upon a bracing wind
Laden with salt and ocean freshness
That dances with the wave tips.
A brisk, cheerful, laughing breeze.
Gone the mindless, raging, howling winds
Tearing at land and sea.
A world renewed, fresh and vigorous
Emerging phoenix-like from turmoil and chaos

09/08/91.

5: WHISPERS

Whispers of lacy wings
Soft flutters through the indigo night
Cool violet moonbeams
Reflect off ebony lakes
Rippled by scarlet saffron moths
Delicately sipping nectar
From miniature lilies of brightest moon-gold

01/03/92

6: DARK SOULS

Dark souls fly through the night
Like winged deamons[2]
Seeking solace within themselves
Finding nothing but dark-fire
Burning like molten brimstone
Coursing through their beings
Fiery claws mercilessly raking them
Writhing in agony immeasurable
They plunge into fathomless wells of darkness
Trying futilely
To slake an unquenchable thirst
To no avail
Till all eternity

27/01/92.

---

[2] Deamons refers to the deamons of Hellenic religion which are benevolent lesser deities and not the malefic demons of Judeo-Christian mythology and theology.

7: EMPTY WELLS

Sorrow weighs heavy upon my heart
i feel the tears within
Welling from deep chambers
The fountain-like spring of my soul
Coursing to spill forth
Cleansing the wounds, healing the pain
But nothing comes
No waters of sorrow are there
The wells are dry
Empty,
But for crimson dust.

10/03/92.

8: DARK BLOOD

The blood runs freely
Dark blood
From the depth of my being
Soul blood
Flowing like a river of fire
Like fire it burns
The essence . . .
There is something that needs to be filled
But the fiery blood
Cannot fill it
[Dominus . . .
  salve me].

22/03/92.

9: RAINDROPS

My heart is empty
But for raindrops
Falling silently

13/05/92.

10: SILVER VELVET

Raindrops fall like tears of joy
From heavens' clouded eyes
Glinting like frozen stars
Heaven's glittering gems,
Glistening with moonlight silver
Upon slick naked flesh
Smooth and taut
To the icy caress of midnight's fingers
Like the gentle flutter of silver velvet moth wings
Gently, gently
Softer that silver silken gossamer threads
Floating upon the night breeze
Lighter than angel kisses
In moonlit magic
To the songs of the stars
In the silence and tumult of souls entwined

09/07/92.

11: COLD STEEL

Cold steel
Bright blade of my dreams
Forbidden key
To the final portal
Emissary of release
To the great unknown
Agent of freedom
Severing bonds and shackles
The final act in life's tragic comedy
Bleak sliver of eternity
Poised to strike
With swift precision
You hesitate
Oh celestial messenger
Guardian of the dark gate
To realms beyond
May i not pass on?
i offer my blood, my essence
Oh drinker of souls
Will you not accept my offering
Am i unworthy
That i may not receive peace
That i may not yet wield
Cold steel

26/08/92.

12: THE GODLESS

The gods have gone
Abandoning the soulless
In a world of blood and chaos
They cry out onto the stars
But no-one answers
Their eyes are filled with fear
Empty hollow fear
They have searched throughout the realms
From the empty pits of Hades
To the barren peaks of Olympus
Finding naught but the wind
And the songs of death
Harsh and shrill keening
Of hollow aching hearts
And empty soulless beings
That wander the earth
Through realms none dare go
In search of divine peace and comfort
Seeking souls and meaning
For their silent sterile existence
The gods watch
And laugh

28/08/92.

13: BURNING SKIES

The sky burned
With the blood of angels
Filling the heavens with fire
Crimson fire
Reaching for the silver sickle moon
And the brilliant blazing stars
In indigo-violet twilight
It burned unto the heavens
With unearthly splendour
As the night cast its dark cloak
Across the gloaming land
Like silent peaceful death descending
Snuffing the embers of fallen seraphim
Staunching the wounds of day
With sleep's soothing hand

30/08/92.

14: STONE ALTAR

i am alone
Before a stone altar to the Gods
Upon barren shores
Of vibrant obsidian
Lapped by crimson waves of blood
And fluorescent pink sea-lace
Blood drains from the dying sun
Filling the ocean's need
Just as the altar drinks the blood of souls
So does the earth
Thirst for the blood of its children
Feeding upon the essence
Of its sacrificial youth
No more than ram offerings
No more death and destruction

03/09/92.

15: DEATH'S SONG

I am darkness
I am death
Take my hand
That you may know peace
I will take you
Beyond pain and fear
Where man's evil
And woman's evil
Cannot be
Take my hand
And let me lead you
Into the shadows of my palace
In the valley of no dreams
Where you may sleep in peace
Forever

12/09/92.

16: THERE IS NO SILENCE

There is no silence
Upon the wind-swept plains
The wind keeps me company
i am not lonely
In the darkness of night
For it envelops me in its cloak
And holds me in its arms
The vast coldness of the universe
Holds no fear for me
The stars are my friends
We speak to our souls alike
i am no more alone
Than a wolf upon a crag
Howling his soul-song
To the cloud-shrouded moon
All Is there with him
Yet he stands alone
Grey and solitary
Caressed by the wind
Son of the night
Heard by the stars
Alone,
Yet not quite
Just separate

24/09/92.

17: DIAMOND STARS FELL

Diamond stars fell
From the ebony moonless sky
Slain by the gods
And my heart was torn in terror
For I knew not what was
No new sun rose to guide me
Not even the fallen stars gave light to darkness
Their shattered fragments
Scattered
Upon an ebony plain
Dead, cold and lifeless
Broken like my soul

. . .

11/09/92.

18: DARK VELVET

Dark velvet are your eyes
Deeper than mist shrouded mysteries
Like molten embers bright
Clear as the midnight starry sky
i could gaze in them
Losing myself deep within their secrets
Discovering the unbound passions
Locked within their depths
i am ensnared, enthralled
By their mysterious power
Seared by their intensity
Their vibrant, potent virility and desire
i cannot, will not resist
Lost am i within your eyes
In your arms
i am safer
Than beneath Archangel wings
Their strength encompass my soul
Gentleness caressing my heart
Drawn within their encirclement; protected
i am content, am peaceful
But for the agony of my heart
As it cries in jubilation
Wanting to leap out into your arms itself
Closer to your heart
My soul is safe
Snuggled warmly, entangled within your limbs
Purring like some great cat
Feline eyes winking; sleepily content
Basking within the warmth of your embrace
If this were death; i would be content
If this is life; i am at peace

20/10/92.

19: DARK HEART

Dark heart
You walk in shadows
In the silence of ebony willows
Weeping by the scarlet water's edge

Why do the shadows follow you
Like haunting shades of twilight?
Dark companions are they
In their sombre silence

The wind blows chill
Through the pines
Dark forests of sorrow
Beneath which we walk

You and i, in silence
Wrapped in grey mantles
Attended by shadow wraiths
Like the wind themselves
Cold and chill
Like the shadows too
Dark and silent; foreboding
Not touching, but passing by
Death-like in the shadowed mist

29/11/92.

20: SOUL SHACKLES

Tell me my friend
Do you hear the wolves
There! howling upon the crags
Deep in the wilderness barren
They call my soul you know
Yes 'tis true i tell you
i hear it stir restlessly
Whining uneasily
Like the caged creature that it is
Eager to be free among its brethren
Wild and gloriously free
But it cannot, cannot
For it is chained, shackled, caged
It howls in despair
In fear, anger and hate
That i should keep it thus
Fettered in chains
Yet 'tis not i, not i
Who commands its entrapment
This foul enslavement
Of wild creature of freedom proud
No 'its not i, but man
Who calls for these burning chains
This crystal palace
No more than a fetid dungeon

21/12/92.

21: THE MOON WEPT

The moon wept dark tears of grief
So too did the stars in sorrow deep and painful
Great indeed was their anguish
Their songs of lament
Great dirges and requiems dark
Filled with pain, horror and fear
Of wrenching sorrow deep
Of these they sang
For this they wept
High in the heavens above
That their children
Those born of shadows and high sorceries
That these of all, men sought
With fear and hatred great
To curse and hunt in anger
Seeking to deny their truth
Their love and beauty scorned, despised
For this the moon and stars wept
That men hunted their children
Simply because they were shadow-born
Born of the moon and stars themselves
Yea, they wept indeed
And still they weep
For mankind's senseless arrogance
Its fear of those different
Of mysteries they know not

21/12/92.

22: BENEATH THE WINGS OF ANGELS

I would walk beneath the wings of angels
Yet I do not
For the skies are filled with fire
And the earth with blood
My brethren slain
Innocents were they
Before men and gods
What justice
Earthly or divine
Holds so little honour
That demons and craven beasts
Would slay and torture innocents
And call it right
Call it just?

12/02/93.

23: NOT MINE

Your eyes are velvet mysteries
Like cool lakes of infinite sorceries
Clear as the midnight sky
With all its starlit splendour
Caught in them
Sparkling with their potent magic dark
Smouldering like the embers in my heart
They burn with dark-fire
Mage-wrought soul power
Your eyes are daggers bright
Plunging into my heart, my soul
Deep i fall into their fathomless mysteries
As my soul cries out in vain
Reaching out blindly for you
To find nothing but darkness
And swirling mists eternal
Cold and empty; silent
Beneath a barren sky
For you are not mine
Not mine and never were

15/03/93.

24: BITTER SALT

i dreamt that we met
Upon a crowded dance floor
You took me in your arms
So strong, so gentle
And kissed me so tenderly
Our tongues entwined, like our souls
Savouring each other's sweetness
Then ...
i licked the slick sweat
Off your sleek taut body
Tasting the bitter salt of your flesh
So smooth and silken
Over graceful feline muscles powerful

18/03/93.

25: BLOOD WILLOWS

Blood willows weeping
Stand upon emerald banks
By the obsidian mirror lake of my soul
Dipping their fingertips and toes
Into its dark waters deep
Sipping their bitter-sweet sorrows
And sighing softly
As the cool gentle night wind
Caresses them, kissing the water's face
Rippling the moonlit, star dusted surface
As it soothes their weeping souls

10/03/93.

26: DRINK DEEP

Your eyes are dark mysteries
Deep shadows, potent, virile
Drinking my soul thirstily
With a fierce burning hunger
Your lips are sweet fire
Branding my flesh with kisses
Fingers tracing searing runes aching
Like fiery trails upon my sweat slicked flesh
i touch your face
A god incarnate's chiselled visage
Agonizingly perfect, powerfully beautiful
Caressed by sable silken hair
Spun of gossamer midnight
Blown like mist about ethereal face
Glowing in starlight silver
As you take me to your soul
That i may drink deep of its waters dark
Deep as you have of mine

23/04/93.

27: LORD OF SORROWS

Speak to me; dominus
Oh lord of sorrows
You of the crimson eyes
Burning with the blood of a million souls
Cloaked in mirrored obsidian robes
Reflecting the darkness of haunted souls
Your silvered wings i see
Stained with scarlet fiery anguish
The sacred blood of tortured hearts
That drains upon that profane altar
Within that unholy temple
They call your own
Tell me dominus
Oh lord of eternal agony
If this be true
Are you a lord of chaos
Who would curse us and laugh
And watch in glee
As your minions of false light
Hunt and slay innocents joyfully
Drunk on the darkness of your wrath (their Hate)
Are you so: dark lord
You speak not
As silent as the death you reek of
Do you not deny this challenge
Mocking me with your silence
Or be those burning tears
Upon your face i see
For those slain in your Name
By false priests and elders
Whom you know not
Nor want to?

29/04/93.

28: WHY DOTH MY SOUL IN AGONY

Why doth my soul in agony
Ache for death
Before it has fully tasted
Life's bitter anguish

05/05/93.

29: BEAUTY

An ivory rose lies trampled
In the sullied snow
A drop of blood
Caught in its heart
Like a crimson ruby bright
Set there in all its tarnished beauty
Still beautiful
As a rose will always be

17/05/93.

30: DARK WINGS

Dark wings obsidian enfold my heart
My soul
In velvet darkness
Sleeps in the crimson cavern of my being
Within the fiery lake of blood and agony
That is the core of my existence
This aching vortex of pain and fearful desire

29/05/93.

31: THE WINE OF YOUR SOUL

Raindrops fall like silver diamonds
Upon the ebony waters of my soul
Will you not touch me
And hold me in your arms
That we may lie limbs entwined
You and i in tender passion deep
Kiss me
For your lips are sweet
And sweeter still
The wine of your soul

30/05/93.

32: WILLING

Your eyes are like the wild gazelle's
Yet piercing like the hawk's
And you tremble colt-like
Under my caress
Your warm flesh is smooth and taut
You move with feline grace
Sleek and lithe, powerfully virile
With silken sinews flowing
Stalking willing prey

23/06/93.

33: SLAYER OF STARS

Thrice cursed
Is the slayer of stars
The burner and mocker of dreams
You would cast me into darkness
You have committed me to emptiness
And would laugh at my heart
You deny my essence, my very being
Commanding me to be another
Of your creation uniform
Disharmonious with my pattern
You would force me
Against my soul

09/08/93.

34: YOUR EYES

Dark, dark
The shadows soft
Fall upon my heart
Gentle flakes of sable snow
Cloak in darkness soft
My burning soul of agony
Pierced by Eros' barbs
Heart weeping molten blood
For eyes so dark and soft
Your eyes
My love

16/08/93.

35: MOLTEN DREAMS

Why do your eyes
So soft and aqueous
Like limpid lakes
Of molten dreams
Burning dark umber silken
Tear my heart so
With each glance
Searing my soul
With gentle laughter
That sparkles tantalisingly

19/09/93.

36: CONTENT

My heart reclines gleefully resplendent
Languishing in your arms
Cheshire-like
Content
For it has tasted of your soul
And of your passion
And finding neither wanting
Has drunk its full

24/09/93.

37: MY HEART IS FIRE

Darkness
My heart is fire
For you have touched me
Dipping your hands into my soul
To drink of its waters dark
Your lips are agony infinite
Searing my essence
In a crimson haze
As you slake your thirst
Upon my being

27/09/93.

38: DARK ORISONS

Dark orisons
Crimson fire and sable blood
Burning aching
i call blood!
Soul-riven
You hear me not dominus
Here upon the burning mountain
Beneath which lies my soul
Hidden
Deep in darkness cold
Deeper than the blood sea
Fed by heavens' burning tears
The molten agony of angels weeping
From which my heart unknowing
Slaked its dire thirst
Now more so, painful

03/10/93.

39: WHY DID YOU KISS ME?

Why did you kiss me
With your mouth
So warm and soft
So deliciously seductive
Awakening from its slumbering
The dark beast of passion
i had chained with iron
Now gone
i must calm its clamouring
For more

29/10/93.

40: FEATHERY THUNDER

Feathery thunder
Wafts through the darkness
Calling me softly
A lullaby
As i float
By the shores of dreams
Soft upon silken waves
And moon-spun sea-mist

22/02/94.

41: ENDLESS SHORES

This morning i woke
In my dreams
To the cry of lonely gulls

Winging upon forgotten horizons
Lost in the mists
And heavy chill
Flowing from the sea

Sharp and biting salt
That pricked my naked flesh

Cold: i shivered
For you were not with me
To face the dawn
That crept from the ocean's depth
Beyond the darkness of the world's edge

Cold and harsh
It revealed my nakedness
To the frozen shores
Grey streaked blue
Icy skies and seas of slate

Cold and barren
But for me
Alone upon these endless shores
Yearning for you
To cloak me in your warmth

22/02/94.

42: GREEN MORNING

Green morning
i wake to your softness
Wet; the grey ocean-sky
Light as velvet moss-wind
Upon my senses
You caress my being
Filling the parched aching of my soul
With your gentle coolness
As rain
To bathe my heart

11/044/94.

43: THE LAND'S BLOOD

Brown;
The land's blood
Into the ocean flows
Draining from scarred slopes
Like pus
From many ragged wounds
Festering

05/05/94.

44: BLUE

Blue,
Great Ocean yonder
My horizons
Exceed your own
Beyond the world's edge
And the abyss of my soul
Further than the spinning spheres
Are the burning fields of my agony
Will you not encompass me
In your cool blueness
And rock me
Into eternal sleep
Within your arms
So soft yet powerful
Within which i could lie
One with you
So . . .
Blue

09/06/94.

45: OCEAN

Misty greys
Lie upon the sea
Like gentle shrouds
Cast about my heart
Soft
So soft
Blending horizons vague
With soothing touch
Of crystal rain
Quiet drops
That fall endlessly
Into the eternity
That you are

23/06/94.

46: DRAGON WAIF

Dragon waif
You sit alone
Upon barren tor
Forsaken child
Of ancient greatness
And mighty prophecies
Lost . . .
You weep
Ebony crimson pearls
The glittering pool
Of your agony
Surrounds you
Silent: scintillating
Testimony to your loneliness
Empty as the great hall
And the dragon throne
At whose foot you sit
Weeping Dreams
[forgotten].
. . .?

24/06/94.

47: ACROSS A CROWDED ROOM

So sleek
You move
A golden panther
Graceful
Silken muscles
Taunting me
Luscious body
Beckoning
effortless
You reek vitality
Virility embodied
Your beauty
Should be immortalised
In eternal marble
But cold stone
Could never
Do you justice
Even should the gods
Grant it movement
Nothing,
Could match
The way you move
Me
Just
Sauntering
Across a crowded room

24/08/94.

48: THE KOOLAUS

Majestic[3]
You rise
Leaping
From the Ocean's depth
Your razor ridges
Slash the sky
That bleeds
Rain
To feed you
And cloak
Your ravaged nakedness
In soothing greens
Resplendent

26/08/94

---

[3] The Koolau's are a mountain range on the Windward side of the island of Oahu, in Hawaii.

49: REMEMBER ME

i think of you
Walking
The streets of LA
With all those handsome men
To beguile you
And wonder
Will you remember
Some young fool
Whose heart
Was given you
On a scrap of parchment ?

01/09/94.

50: MY HEART

You held
My heart
In the palm of your hand
And knew it not
All the while
It lay
Quietly
Fearful
You would notice
How intensely
It needed you
To notice it.

03/09/94.

ACKNOWLEDGEMENTS

I'd like to thank all those who read *Dragon Waif* during its compilation and preparation for publication, especially those who read my other "sketches" during the early years while I was a student at James Cook University and encouraged me to keep writing.

In particular I'd like to give special thanks to: Adriana Peters and Ian Moles for reading, catching typos and constructive criticism even if I did not always take the advice given; Clem Matheson for the poetic license to use "irridiant". I still have the "official poetic license" you gave me on file, stashed away safely; Wade J. Mullings for being my first flat mate at Uni and surprising my other friends by greeting them at the door of our flat in his boxer shorts; Fiona Shon, Catherine Cantarella and Ludmilla Solonda for reading my poetry over cappuccino with fish and chips between French lectures at James Cook University; Marcelléa Roest-Bonestroo, Marilou Gutierrez, Jacqui Garza, Pearce Nelson, Dayan Cronin, Deborah Sue, Erich Volschenk, Jason Russo, Gary Seah, Annie Low, Ben Chang, Helen Tanuvasa and Matilda Bartley also for reading; Belinda Rose Veivers for writing a poem about me and reading my poetry and attempts at science fiction and fantasy; Pam Paramjeet Kaur for reading my poetry and sharing her poems with me and Rey Ileto for saying he's never had a "Poet" in one of his classes before; Charlotte Chan Mow, Jerry Brunt, Fiti Leung Wa and Jason Bebrouth for their interest and support in my efforts to get my poetry published.

Thanks also to: Brenda Latu-Heather for reading and sharing my poetry with others in the Attorney General's Office and telling them I was a poet; Vincent L. Fasone Jr. for restoring my faith in the innate kindness and goodness of people and being kind and generous to strangers in distress as well as for his moral support, kindness and friendship, over the years and Joe Meyers for reading my poems and commissioning one from me as well as letting me stay with his family in Mililani, Hawaii.

I also want to thank: Mrs Sue Rasmussen for reading my very early attempts at science fiction and fantasy and for encouraging me to write, way back when I was still in high school, even though she was not my teacher; my English teachers at Samoa College and the National University of Samoa: Miss VandenDriesen, Mrs Kolose, Mrs Barlow, Mrs. Emma Kruse-Vaai and Mrs Sina Vaai.

I would also like to thank Laulu Lolesio Tevaga, the Government Printer for his patience and taking the time to answer my questions about the offset printing process and preparation of print ready masters and esoteric things like margins even though I was only supposed to be following up on the status of the printing of the government's budget documents and not be getting an introduction to the offset printing process. Likewise I must thank Makerita Vaai of the University of the South Pacific's Malifa Library and Mataina Te'o of the Nelson Memorial Library who were helpful in my very early efforts to learn about copyright law and the publication process when I was at Leif'ifi Intermediate and Samoan College. Mataina also rescued me from spending a weekend locked in the library.

I must also thank: Mrs Lynne Enari and my aunt Christine Quested for offering advice on what to include in the "About the author" section; Claire Lepack and Sonny Mulitalo for their advice on how to resolve certain bank conundrums that were proving an obstacle to being able to set things up for Iland Ink Publishing to be able to start publishing; my cousins Hinauri Petana and Unutoa Auelua for confirming Laulu, Makerita and Mataina's full names for me and Caroline Applin for the chocolates and Monte Carlos sent to Belgium all the way from Australia.

I would also like to acknowledge and give special thanks to my aunt and uncle: Jan and Tom Reyes as well as one of my best friends and former flatmate: Wade J. Mullings for their financial assistance without which the publication of this book would not have been possible. Thank you so much. I really appreciate your support and faith in me.

I must also thank the late Ms Mable Howse of Leifi'ifi Intermediate School for introducing me to writing poetry. You planted a seed long ago with a single poetry writing exercise and I am sad that you did not get to see its flowering let alone its fruits.

And to Martin Saker and Brett Page: for just being.

Blessed Be.

Vincent A. Matatumua Vermeulen,

Brussels BELGIUM.

ABOUT THE POET

Born in Hawaii, Vincent A. Matatumua Vermeulen also known as Vincent A. Vermeulen grew up in Samoa. His education began at Saint Theresa's Catholic School and was continued briefly in Belgium and the United Kingdom. Upon returning to Samoa he completed his primary and secondary education at Apia Primary School, Leifi'ifi Intermediate School and Samoa College.

He commenced his tertiary studies at the National University of Samoa where he completed his University Preparatory Year Certificate and was awarded an AusAid Scholarship to study at James Cook University in Townsville, Queensland, Australia.

Following the completion of a Bachelor of Arts degree in Australia he commenced working in the Samoan Civil Service first in the Treasury/Ministry of Finance and then in the Ministry of Foreign Affairs and Trade, leaving occasionally to live in Hawaii as well as to pursue postgraduate studies at the University of Sydney in New South Wales, Australia, the Katholike Universiteit Leuven in Flemish Brabant, Belgium and the University of Bristol in the United Kingdom.

From a young age Vincent grew to love reading, so much that he was became a regular visitor at the Nelson Memorial Library in Apia and often was given special dispensation to stay in the children's section in the mezzanine after the Children's section closed. This led to him getting accidentally locked into the Library one Friday evening when librarians forgot he was there. His introduction to the writing of poetry was at Leifi'ifi Intermediate School through his English Teacher the late redoubtable Ms Mable Howse. However, although he did write a few poems that were published in the Samoa College News Bulletin, it was not until at James Cook University that he started writing poetry in earnest. He had some poetry selections (along with some articles on history and politics) published in the Magnus Taurus and others in The Orphean.

NOTES TO THIS EDITION

In some ways this edition is the third but the first published and made available to the public. In 1995 I had twenty copies printed and bound at a copy shop, which I gave to some friends and family members while I was living in Honolulu, Hawaii. Then in 2002 I had another five copies made while I was in Sydney, Australia. Again, I gave them to some friends and family. Each "edition" contained revisions; mainly corrections to typographical errors as well as a different cover design and cover artwork.

This edition is first official edition intended for public consumption contains significant changes to the form of the poetry. Perhaps one of the most significant has been the inclusion of titles. Although I originally started using titles I abandoned their use half way through *Empty Wells*, the second volume of *Sketches from the Other Side of My Soul*. Latter I designated roman numerals to each poem prefixed by the volume number based on the order that they had been written in.

I also ceased to use capitals except in very specific instances. This was because to me a capital letter indicated the start of a new sentence. The problem that I saw with this was that in some cases depending on how one read them, there were poems in which one could actually read (for example) line one and two as a complete sentence as well as line two and three and in the same sense line three and four, all as separate sentences. That is lines one to four could not be read as one sentence but each line could in some way form part of the preceding or subsequent line. I felt at the time that capitals would preclude the ability of readers to see and appreciate this.

Another important reason for my decision to not use capitals was because of the letter 'i'. By using a small "i" for the personal pronoun I was seeking to impart a sense of diminishing the importance of the self as in the self, had become so diminished that it no longer merited a capital letter.

This aspect has been retained to the chagrin of the spell check program. One factor which made me reconsider the lack of capitals is that someone assumed that I was imitating e. e. cummings and I did not appreciate that assumption. Not because I do not like e. e. cummings but because I do not like the thought of anyone assuming I was copying someone else's style. However, it is a logical assumption but I decided to just leave things as they are for most of the poems.

I have however, made some changes to the wording of some poems as well as changing their structure to some extent. Some of this has been due to trying to fit some poems onto a page. However, I tried to refrain as much as possible from too much editing as I have always felt that in the case of these poems that the original flow of thoughts and words had been captured in the form most reflective of the thoughts and emotions that generated them.

The second lot of books printed was supposed to have illustrations in it. These were intended to ensure that poems that extended over two pages would end up opening up side by side rather than on different sides of the same leaf. I could have shuffled poems about to ensure that this happened but wanted to retain the order in which they were written. In reality any importance or insight to be gained by retaining chronological order is lost in any case because the selection was made from the first fifteen volumes of Sketches from the Other side of My Soul and as such the chronology is skewed as interposing poems are missing. This was clearly evident to anyone who notes the numbering and dates.

Another minor change I have made is that I have added one additional poem to bring the total included in the collection to 50. Although I originally considered adding one from the existing volumes I ended up including "Rain" which was the very first poem I wrote as part of a class I took with the redoubtable and unforgettable Miss Howse who taught several generations of students at Leifi'ifi Intermediate School. I later added additional stanzas to it for publication in one of the editions of the Samoa College School Bulletin in 1983 but I decided that in honour of Ms. House I would include it in its shorter original form.

One other major change is that of the name under which it was published under. Originally I had wanted to use the pseudonym Nikolai Alexsandrov as the pen name under which to publish my poetry. In the end I settled on Darum which is what is on the cover of the 1st and 2nd 'editions'. Part of the reason for my wanting to use a pseudonym is that there are many very dark poems included. That is poems dealing with death, depression and suicide. In addition there are a number love poems that I was worried about how people would react negatively to.

This edition is published under the name Vincent A. Matatumua Vermeulen. I was going to publish it under the shorter Vincent A. Vermeulen rather than using the double barrelled surname which can cause confusion for some people. But while doing some searches for something else I discovered that there was already at least one author named Vincent Vermeulen.

So in order to avoid any confusion I've decided to publish under Vincent A. Matatumua Vermeulen which in order to fit on the book cover has been shortened to V. A. Matatumua Vermeulen on the cover. Incidentally while I was at James Cook University I published quite a few poems in the weekly *Bullsheet* as well as the monthly *Magnus Taurus*. All these were published under Vincent A. Matatumua Vermeulen, so this ensures both less confusion as well as some continuity.

ABOUT ISLAND INK PUBLISHING

Island Ink Publishing is a small independent publishing house. We publish poetry, including collections, pamphlets and the occasional anthology; fiction, including novels, novellas and collections of short stories; non-fiction, including history, law, botany, memoirs and travel writing; lexicons, including bilingual and multilingual dictionaries as well as phrasebooks and botanical lexicons; language acquisition material, including dual language texts, language learning books and other learning and teaching materials.

We also publish out of print classic and heritage works of academic, cultural, historical and literary importance, including fiction, non-fiction, poetry, lexicons and compilations of documents; and translations of various works, including classical and heritage works.

Island Ink Publishing Company Limited is also interested in finding and promoting new authors. We are especially interested in fiction by own voice authors especially, but not limited to authors of minority and marginalized communities. We are also interested in fiction portraying characters of minority and marginalized communities as protagonists and or major characters in strong positive role as well as works dealing with issues related to such communities.

Although we mainly publish books in English and French, we also publish books in other languages and are always seeking to extend our range of languages.

Please visit our website to find out more about us, what books we have available and what our submission guidelines are.

SKETCHES FROM THE OTHER SIDE OF MY SOUL

Sketches from the Other Side of My Soul currently comprises the following volumes:

Venusian Mysteries	Volume 1	1990-1991
Empty Wells	Volume 2	1992
Silver Velvet	Volume 3	1992
Stone Tower	Volume 4	1992
Mirror of My Soul	Volume 5	1992
Prince of Shadows	Volume 6	1992
Shadow Born	Volume 7	1992
Dark Eyes	Volume 8	1993
Adsum Domine	Volume 9	1993
Blood and Shadows	Volume 10	1993
Moth Heart	Volume 11	1993
Dark Orisons	Volume 12	1993
Dream Spinner	Volume 13	1994
Ice Lord	Volume 14	1994
Napalm Cocktails	Volume 15	1994-1995
Diamond Kisses	Volume 16	1995
Anemones in the Wind	Volume 17	1995-1996
Ashes	Volume 18	1996-1999
Like Icarus	Volume 19	2000
Dark Eternity	Volume 20	2000-2001
Dark Flight	Volume 21	2001 – 2020
Blood Song	Volume 22	2020 -

OTHER WORKS BY THE AUTHOR

Dragon Waif. A Selection of Sketches from the Other Side of My Soul: comprised of selections from the first 15 Volumes of Sketches from the Other Side of My Soul.
ISBN - 978-1-914093-00-5 Paperback edition.
ISBN - 978-1-914093-01-2 Hard Cover edition.

Heart Ink. A Selection of Sketches from the Other Side of My Soul: comprised of selections from the first 20 Volumes of Sketches from the Other Side of My Soul.
ISBN - 978-1-914093-02-9 Paperback edition.
ISBN - 978-1-914093-03-6 Hard Cover edition.

Sketches from the Other Side of My Soul Volumes 1 – 5
ISBN - 978-1-914093-04-3 Hard Cover edition

Sketches from the Other Side of My Soul Volumes 6 – 10
ISBN - 978-1-914093-05-0 Hard Cover edition

Sketches from the Other Side of My Soul Volumes 11 – 15
ISBN - 978-1-914093-06-7 Hard Cover edition

Sketches from the Other Side of My Soul Volumes 16 – 20
ISBN - 978-1-914093-07-4 Hard Cover edition

Venusian Mysteries. Sketches from the Other Side of My Soul Volume 1
ISBN -978-1-914093-09-8 Paperback edition
Empty Wells. Sketches from the Other Side of My Soul Volume 2
ISBN - 978-1-914093-10-4 Paperback edition
Silver Velvet. Sketches from the Other Side of My Soul Volume 3
ISBN - 978-1-914093-11-1 Paperback edition
Stone Tower. Sketches from the Other Side of My Soul Volume 4
ISBN - 978-1-914093-12-8 Paperback edition
Mirror of My Soul. Sketches from the Other Side of My Soul Volume 5
ISBN - 978-1-914093-13-5 Paperback edition
Prince of Shadows. Sketches from the Other Side of My Soul Volume 6
ISBN - 978-1-914093-14-2 Paperback edition
Shadow Born. Sketches from the Other Side of My Soul Volume 7
ISBN - 978-1-914093-15-9 Paperback edition
Dark Eyes. Sketches from the Other Side of My Soul Volume 8
ISBN - 978-1-914093-16-6 Paperback edition
Adsum Domine. Sketches from the Other Side of My Soul Volume 9
ISBN - 978-1-914093-17-3Paperback edition
Blood and Shadows. Sketches from the Other Side of My Soul Volume 10
ISBN - 978-1-914093-18-0 Paperback edition
Moth Heart. Sketches from the Other Side of My Soul Volume 11
ISBN - 978-1-914093-19-7 Paperback edition
Dark Orisons. Sketches from the Other Side of My Soul Volume 12
ISBN - 978-1-914093-20-3 Paperback edition
Dream Spinner. Sketches from the Other Side of My Soul Volume 13
ISBN - 978-1-914093-21-0 Paperback edition
Ice Lord. Sketches from the Other Side of My Soul Volume 14
ISBN - 978-1-914093-22-7 Paperback edition
Napalm Cocktails. Sketches from the Other Side of My Soul Volume 15
ISBN - 978-1-914093-23-4 Paperback edition
Diamond Kisses. Sketches from the Other Side of My Soul Volume 16
ISBN - 978-1-914093-24-1 Paperback edition
Anemones in the Wind. Sketches from the Other Side of My Soul Volume 17
ISBN - 978-1-914093-25-8 Paperback edition
Ashes. Sketches from the Other Side of My Soul Volume 18
ISBN - 978-1-914093-26-5 Paperback edition
Like Icarus. Sketches from the Other Side of My Soul Volume 19
ISBN - 978-1-914093-27-2 Paperback edition
Dark Eternity. Sketches from the Other Side of My Soul Volume 20
ISBN - 978-1-914093-28-9 Paperback edition
Dark Flight. Sketches from the Other Side of My Soul Volume 21
ISBN - 978-1-914093-29-6 Paperback edition .

Published by Hyacinthus Books™ an imprint of
Island Ink Publishing Company Limited, 71-75 Shelton Street,
Covent Garden, London, WC2H 9JQ, UNITED KINGDOM

Typeset in Garamond 36 and 18 point.
Perpetua Titling MT 14 and 11 point
Calibri 11 point
Verdana 10 and 8 point
Typesetting, layout and design by Dioskouri Designs

Cover image www.Canva.com

Island Ink Publishing Co. Ltd.